Iris Niebac

TATTED DOILIES

Akacia

Drawings: Iris Niebach

Forlaget Akacia
Skovvænget 1
DK-5690 Tommerup
akacia@akacia.dk

First print: 2004
Second print: 2008
Printed at Dardedze Holografija, Riga

Even though both the author of the present book and the staff at the publishing house try to make a book without any errors, we have to admit that is not always possible to do so - especially not whith craft books. If you should find any errors in this book that is of significance for making the designs, please do not hesitate to contact the publisher. Any corrections may then be seen at the homepage of Forlaget Akacia www.akacia.dk

ISBN: 87-7847-081-1
ISBN: 978-87-7847-081-2

INTRODUCTION

For those of us who love handwork, there is nothing more satisfying than making a beautiful doily, and these small doilies need only a little time.

And how do we use a doily, other than placing it on the table under decorative items?
We can sew it on to a silk or velvet cushion. It can be framed and hung on the wall or used as an insertion in a pillow slip, curtain or tablecloth. It can be worked in very thin yarn and placed on a little box covered with fabric or joined with others to make a bigger tablecloth. There are plenty of possibilities. And last, our friends and relatives will be happy to receive it as a present.

In this book there is one traditional doily and a couple of ovals, which are done in more rounds, but most of the doilies can be completed in only one round. This makes only a few ends to hide.

I have tried to make the diagrams as clear as possible and I hope they are understandable. The starting point and the direction of the work on the diagrams are indicated with arrows to make it easier to work and to finish the doilies. I like to keep the doilies simple, and therefore there are few picots, and most often these picots are used for joinings. If you want to sew the doily on a cushion or use it as an insertion you can add some picots in the appropriate places.

I hope you will get as much pleasure with these doilies as I have had designing and working them out, and that I experience every time I work one of them.

Iris Niebach

SYMBOLS

Ring with picot

Chain with picot

Joining picot
Step-by-step instructions on page 5

Change the shuttles after a chain and work - after a joining picot - the next chain in opposite direction.

Josephine knot
All the Josephine knots in this book have 12 half knots.

The arrow indicates that 'chain, ring and chain' should be worked.

A number inside a ring indicates the number of double knots between the picots.

Numbers between rings - or between ring and chain - apply to both sides: that means the lower knots in the rings and the upper part of the chain.

Change shuttles at S.

Double picot
Make a large picot and the given amounts of double knots. Crochet the picot down. With a crochet hook the picot is formed to look like a small picot surrounded by a bigger one.

O   This ring indicates a joining picot and changing the direction of a chain - without working a ring.

a, b, c   Small letters beside arrows indicate the order of the tatted elements.

◀   A little triangle indicates that at this point there no joining picot, but only a little space between knots to join.

O   O besides an 'onion' indicates that the inner ring has to be done by the working tread.

U   U besides an 'onion' indicates that the inner ring has to be done by the core tread.

Remark that long chains tend to twist. To avoid this work the chain and the folowing ring, then with thumb and index finger pass over the knots of the chain to distribute them evenly.

Joining picot, step-by-step

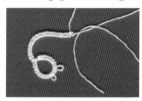

1. Put a thread inside the chain on the place where you intend to join. Work as normal.

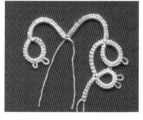

2. To be able to join with the core thread, pull out a picot and take away the inlaid thread.

3. Join with the picot as usual and work on according the diagram.

AMANDA

Dimension: 22 cm in diameter
2 shuttles
Crochet hook no. 0,70
Yarn no. 30

Make the doily in one round according the diagram.
Start with the ring at START
and work in the directions
of the arrows. After 'j'
go on to 'e'.
Be aware that the
picots between
the small rings
of the flowers
have to be
about 4
mm.

START

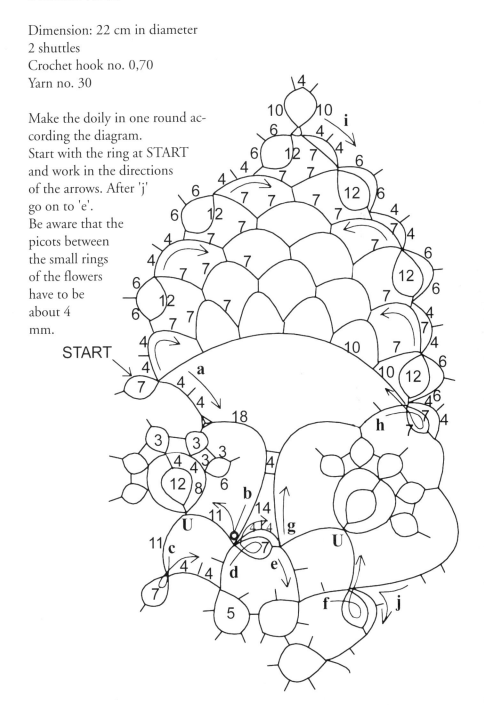

BEATRICE

Dimension: 20 cm in diameter
1 shuttle + ball thread
Crochet hook no. 1,00
Yarn no. 20

Make the doily in one round according the diagram.
Start with the ring at START.

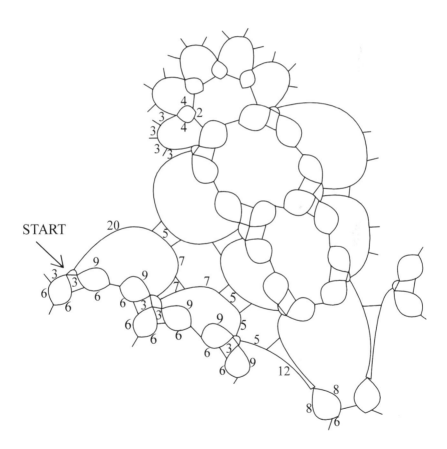

CORNELIA

Dimension: 18 cm in diameter
1 shuttle + ball thread
Crochet hook no. 0,60
Yarn no. 40

Make the doily in one round according the diagram.
Start with the ring at START.

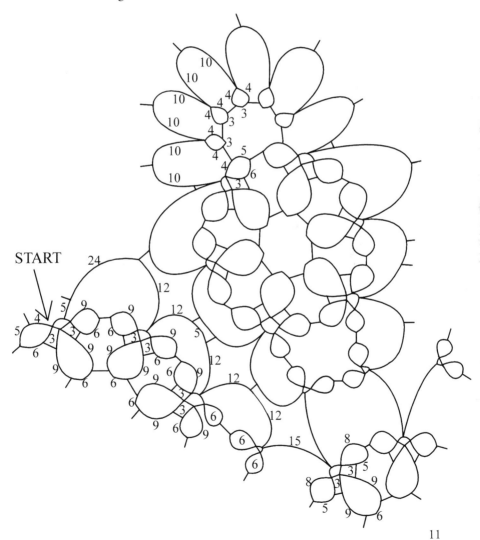

DELIA

Dimension: 19,5 cm in diameter
2 shuttles
Crochet hook no. 0,60
Yarn no. 40

Make the doily in one round according
the diagram.
Start with the ring at START and follow
the arrows carefully. After 'n' go on to 'd'.

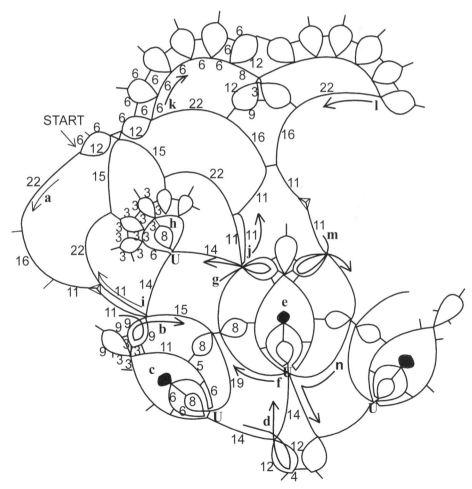

ELEONORA

Dimension: 18,5 cm in diameter
2 shuttles
Crochet hook no. 1,00
Yarn no. 20

Make the doily in one round according the diagram.
Start with the ring at START.
Regarding the joining picot look at the step-by-step pohotos on page 5.

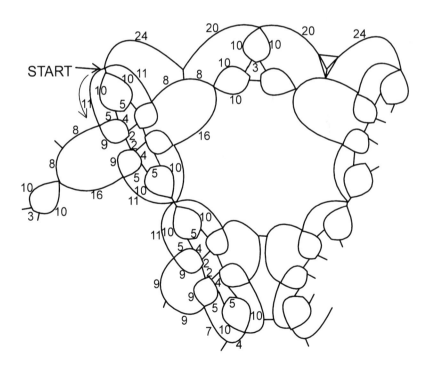

FRANCESCA

Dimension: 21 cm in diameter
2 shuttles
Crochet hook no. 0,70
Yarn no. 30

Make the doily in one round according the diagram.
Start with the chain at START, thereby a little picot is formed.
Be aware that the picots between the small rings of the flowers have to be a little bigger than normal.

START

GRACIELLA

Dimensions: 26 x 15 cm
2 shuttles
Crochet hook no. 0,60
Yarn no. 20

Make the doily in five rounds according the diagram.
Start with the ring at START. The chain with rings
of the floweredge has to be worked backwards.
Be aware that the picots
between the small rings of
the flowers have to be
4-5 mm.
The center alone is
a fine, little doily.

4.Rnd

3.Rnd

2.Rnd

START

19

IRENE

Dimensions: 17 x 9,6 cm
2 shuttles
Crochet hook no. 0,60
Yarn no. 40

Make the doily in two rounds according the diagram.
Start with the chain at START, thereby a little picot is formed.
Work backwards. After 'i' go on to the starting chain.

START

2. Rnd

21

LORELLA

Dimension: 19 cm in diameter
2 shuttles
Crochet hook no. 0,70
Yarn no. 30

Make the doily in one round according the diagram.
Start with the chain at START, thereby a little picot is formed. Work in the direction of the arrows. After 'e' go on to 'a'.

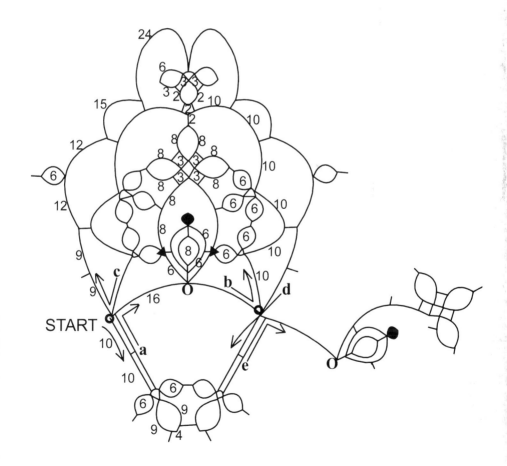

MILENA

Dimension: 19 cm in diameter
2 shuttles
Crochet hook no. 1,00
Yarn no. 40

Make the doily in one round according the
diagram.
Start with the ring at START and work
in the direction of the arrows.
After 'f' go on to 'a'.

NORA

Dimension: 20 cm in diameter
2 shuttles for the first round
1 shuttle + ball thread for the following rounds
Crochet hook no. 1,00
Yarn no. 40

Make the doily in 5 rounds according the diagram.
3. round: Start with the chain, that makes it easier to
finish the round.

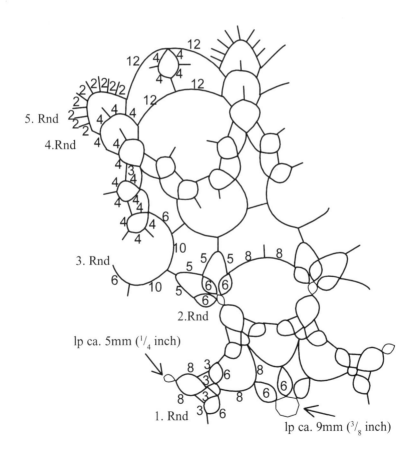

ANNALISA

Dimensions: 19 x 19 cm
2 shuttles
Crochet hook no. 0,70
Yarn no. 30

Make the doily in one round according the diagram. Remark that the diagrams for A, B and C are on page 30. Start with the chain at START, thereby a little picot is formed. Work in the direction of the arrows. Arrived at 'o' return to 'a'.
The square shape gives the opportunity for several different doilies - here three of them are shown.

START

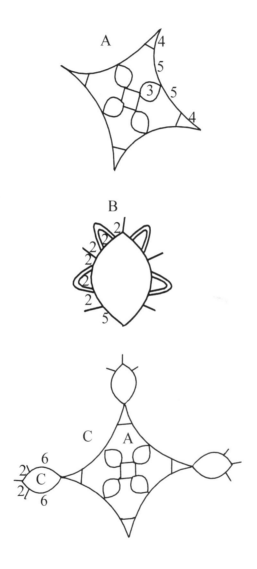

ANNAMARIA

Variation of Annalisa on page 28

ANNARITA

Variation of Annalisa on page 28